W9-BJC-206

FACE
TO FACE
WITH
SCIENCE™

*The Search
for the
Right Whale*

*Scott Kraus & Kenneth Mallory*

A New England Aquarium Book
CROWN PUBLISHERS, INC., *New York*

Published by Crown Publishers, Inc., a Random House
company, 201 East 50th Street, New York, New York
10022

CROWN is a trademark of Crown Publishers, Inc.
Manufactured in Hong Kong

Library of Congress Cataloging-in-Publication Data
Kraus, Scott D.
The search for the right whale / by Scott Kraus and
Kenneth Mallory.
p.  cm.
Includes index.
Summary: Follows a team of New England Aquarium
scientists as they follow and study migrating North Atlantic
right whales and speculates about the future survival of
this endangered species.
1. Whales—North Atlantic Ocean—Juvenile literature. 2.
Whale watching—North Atlantic Ocean—Juvenile
literature. [1. Whales—North Atlantic Ocean. 2. Whale
watching. 3. Rare animals. 4. Wildlife conservation.] I.
Mallory, Kenneth. II. Title.
QL737.C4K73  1993
599.5'1—dc20                              92-18091

ISBN  0-517-57844-1 (trade)
         0-517-57845-X (lib. bdg.)

10 9 8 7 6 5 4 3

Photographs on pages 9 (*bottom*), 24, 25, 33 (*bottom*) ©
Doug Allan/Oxford Scientific Films; 6 (*left*) © Camille
Vickers; 12 & 13, The Kendall Whaling Museum, Sharon,
Massachusetts, U.S.A.; 16 (*right*) & 17, from the collection
of The Vineyard Museum/Dukes County Historical Society,
Edgartown, Massachusetts. All other photographs © The
New England Aquarium. Photographers: pages 2-3, 10
(*top*): Moira Brown; 30 (*right*): Kevin Chu; 7 (*top*), 34: Jackie
Ciano; 22 (*inset*): Martie J. Crone; 9 (*top left*): Steve
Dawson; 18: Nancy Gunnlaugsson; 14 (*right*): Brian Hoover;
28 (*left*): David James; 14 (*left*), 28-29, 29: Amy Knowlton;
5 (*right*), 7 (*bottom*), 8 (*inset*), 16 (*center left and bottom
left*), 30 (*left*), 31, 33 (*top*): Scott D. Kraus; 5 (*top left,
center left, bottom left*): Paula McKay; 4 (*left*): Ken Mallory;
9 (*top right*): Karen Payne; 23: Jana Pennington; 4(*top right
and bottom right*), 11, 20, 22: John H. Prescott; 6 (*right*), 8
(*bottom*), 10 (*bottom*), 21, 26: Chris Slay; 1, 15 (*left and
center*): Greg Stone; 15 (*right*): Porter Turnbull.

Illustration on page 9 by Sarah Landry © The New England
Aquarium

Maps by Anne Diebel.

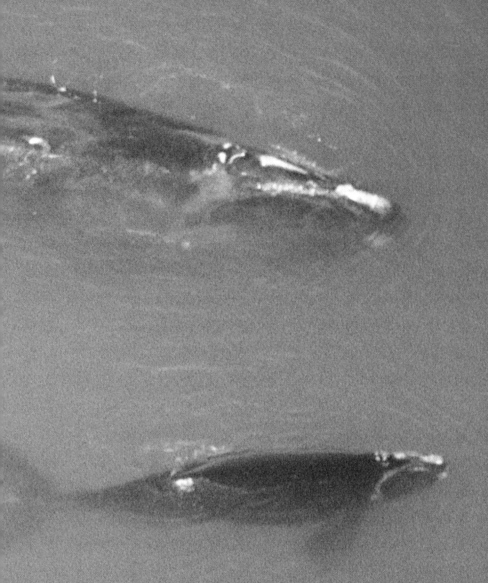

*It is a cold* and breezy morning late in September 1991. More than ten miles off the coast of Nova Scotia, a dark shape breaks the surface of the North Atlantic Ocean. It makes a loud whooshing sound, like a fierce wind blowing across the opening of a large, wide pipe. Clouds of spray shoot up toward the sky in a watery mist.

A North Atlantic right whale named Stripe has just surfaced for a breath of air. At first, Stripe floats motionless and alone. Salt water washes over her back, making ripples and tiny waves. Seconds later, she is joined at the surface by another whale, this one half her size.

▲ ▼ Stripe. The long white scar on top of her head gave Stripe her name.

My name is Scott Kraus. As leader of a team of scientists from the New England Aquarium in Boston, Massachusetts, I am just 500 feet away, watching Stripe and her baby, called a "calf," with a pair of binoculars. At 30 feet long, our research boat, the **Nereid**, is only slightly longer than Stripe's calf.

We are surveying a small group of the rarest whale in the ocean, the North Atlantic right whale. The survey is part of a long-term study designed to obtain information that will ensure the survival of right whales. Together with other scientists, we are keeping track of as many individual whales as we can—trying to learn where they live, what they eat, and what can be done to protect them. By 1991, we have been following some whales for over ten years.

4

Stripe is one of our oldest friends. Her name comes from the long scar on the top of her head. We can only guess how Stripe got the scar. It may have been caused by a collision with a boat. Or she may have crashed into the bottom of the ocean while chasing food.

On Stripe's head, there are strange-looking patches of raised rough skin called **callosities**. Callosities provide a home for whale lice—tiny animals less than an inch long that look like crabs—but no one knows why right whales have the callosities. They look like gray and white islands against the whale's shiny black skin. Callosity patterns appear in the same places a person might have a mustache, a beard, and eyebrows.

These odd skin patches help researchers like me tell one right whale from another. The callosities on each individual whale form different patterns, like fingerprints. They remain more or less the same throughout the whale's life.

◀ Three views of the same whale, showing callosities on the *bonnet*, or top of the head, on the lower lip, and around the blowhole.

▶ Whale lice shown next to a centimeter ruler.

▲ Aboard the *Nereid,* Scott Kraus (*center, with beard*) and Amy Knowlton (*on far right edge*).

*Right:* Photographing a surfacing whale.

As we approach the two floating whales, our research team begins collecting data. Although it sounds like total confusion, it is, in fact, a carefully planned routine.

"Two islands right!" (Meaning: two callosity islands on the whale to the right.)

"CKS, twelve, frames three to seven!" ("CKS" are the observer's initials; "twelve" refers to film roll number 12; and "frames three to seven" are the numbers of the photographs taken by the observer.)

"Lips?" (Meaning: are there callosities on the lower lips?)

"Look, continuous post blowholes!" (The callosities are joined behind the blowholes.)

"Oh! Did you get that headlift?"

"Yes, ARK, ten, frames 21 through 26!"

"Any mud?"

"Aargh, I'm out of film!"

This apparent chaos provides the record keeper with information about the identifying features and photographs taken of each whale. Teamwork is essential.

▲ The mud on a whale's nose may be an indication of deep diving in search of food.

Another thing we notice is mud on Stripe's nose. It is evidence that right whales make deep dives to the ocean bottom in search of food. Sometimes Stripe gets so carried away she runs right into the ocean bottom and ends up with mud on her head.

While Stripe has been searching for something to eat, her young calf appears to have become bored. A tangled crown of seaweed is draped around his head like a brown and green beret. Right whale calves are no different from any other animal youngster: they love to play. Pushing a little seaweed around may give the calf something to do.

▼ Playing with seaweed.

During our encounter with Stripe and her calf, we take photos, record behavior, and collect samples of skin using small darts shot from a crossbow. The pieces of skin and blubber help us determine how the whales are related to each other. They also tell us if the whale is healthy, since pollutants show up in the blubber.

We are excited to see Stripe swimming with a calf. From our own sightings and from earlier records made by other scientists, we know this is her sixth baby in the last 25 years. Later that day, as we drift with the **Nereid**'s engines turned off, we recognize one of Stripe's grownup calves, Stars, accompanied by a baby of her own. We met Stars as a newborn calf back in 1981. We gave her the name because the callosities on her head looked like clusters of stars. Stars' calf is her second, making Stripe a grandmother for the second time.

▼ A whale with a dart in its back. The line used to retrieve the dart can be seen trailing behind. The shot is painless. The inset shows three of the small darts used to collect blubber and skin from whales.

▲ Two pictures of Stars: her head, with star-like clusters of callosities (*left*) and the jagged white pattern on her belly (*right*).

## About the Right Whale

The North Atlantic right whale, *Eubalaena glacialis*, ranges from 45 to 55 feet in length and can weigh up to 70 tons. Females usually grow larger than males. Both are black in color, often with patches of white on their throats and bellies. Their large heads, with narrow upper jaw and strongly bowed lower jaw, take up more than a quarter of their body length. Two widely separated blowholes make a distinctive V-shaped spout when seen from the front or back, making it easy to spot right whales from a distance. They have no dorsal fin, and their flukes, or tail fins, are broad and deeply notched. A closely related species, the southern right whale, *Eubalaena australis*, lives in the oceans of the southern hemisphere from Brazil to the Antarctic. Southern right whales are more numerous than North Atlantic right whales.

▲ An underwater photograph of a southern right whale. North Atlantic and southern right whales are very similar in looks and behavior. It is difficult to photograph North Atlantic right whales underwater because of murkier water in their habitat.

A week later, a third member of the family, Forever, appears swimming by herself. We first saw Forever as a newborn calf in the winter of 1984. She is Stripe's fourth calf, the next one after Stars. Forever doesn't have any easily identified features, so we broke with tradition: instead of naming her for distinctive markings, we named her so that together the names of the mother and her calves would have a special meaning. To us, the family of "Stars and Stripes Forever" symbolized our hopes for the rebirth of the North Atlantic right whale.

◀ ▲ Forever.

CANADA

UNITED
STATES

10

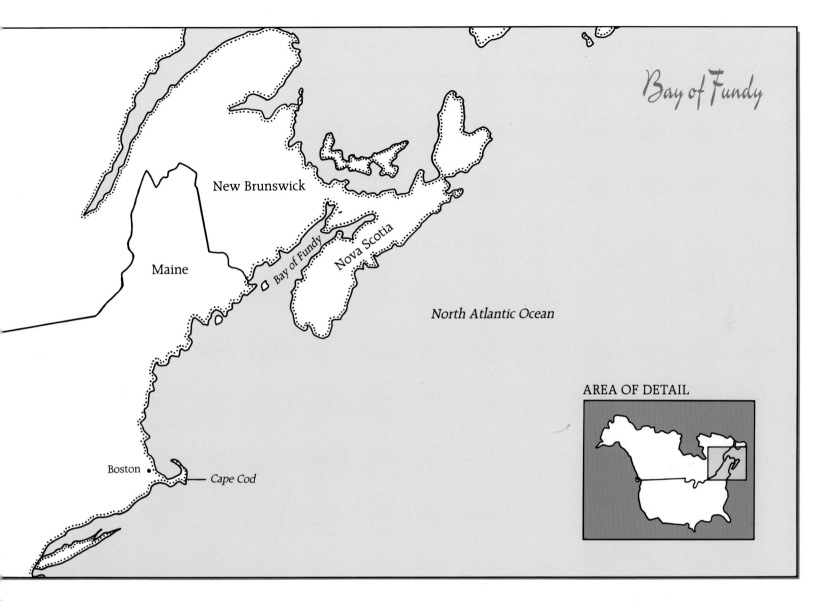

Bay of Fundy

New Brunswick

Maine

Bay of Fundy

Nova Scotia

North Atlantic Ocean

Boston

Cape Cod

AREA OF DETAIL

▼ Coast of the Bay of Fundy.

*Our study* of the North Atlantic right whale began in 1980, when the New England Aquarium was asked to conduct a survey of the marine mammals in the Bay of Fundy, an area between New Brunswick and Nova Scotia. An oil company planned to place a refinery in the bay. They wanted to know what impact the building of a large tanker port might have on the surrounding wildlife. To our great surprise, we discovered 26 different right whales during our survey, including four mothers with their calves. Fortunately, the refinery was never built.

The right whale got its name because it was the "right" whale for people who hunted whales. It swam slowly at the surface, so it was easy to catch and kill. Once killed, it floated—making retrieval easy—instead of sinking out of sight. And when it was boiled, the right whale's foot-thick layer of blubber produced as many as 70 barrels of lamp and lubricating oil.

▼ *The Whale Fishery*, a colored aquatint, shows the crew of an early nineteenth-century whale boat attempting to harpoon a right whale. In the background, other whalemen are raising the *blanket piece*, a large piece of blubber they have peeled from the body of the whale and attached to a blubber hook. It is raised onto the ship by pumping the *windlass*, a winch that was also used to raise and lower the anchor. The smoke comes from the giant-size pots of the *tryworks*, or on-deck furnace, where blubber cut into small pieces was rendered into oil.

This colored line engraving, entitled *A Whale Female and the Windlais Whereby the Whales Are Brought on Shore*, shows a right whale being processed on shore in the year 1619. The *lemmer*, or worker who butchered the whale, is standing on the whale using a flensing tool to cut the blanket piece of blubber. In the foreground are winches used to hoist the whale. The whale's baleen plates, which are hanging from its mouth, were highly flexible and were used to make corsets, buggy whips, strapping for beds, umbrella stays, and caning for chairs, and when properly tanned could be molded into items such as spoons and soup ladles. Baleen was also carved and used to inlay decorative box covers, combs, and brushes. The soft, fine fringe lining on the inside of the baleen plate was used to stuff mattresses and chairs, and also to make wigs.

For over 900 years, beginning about the year A.D. 1000, whaling nations from Europe and America hunted North Atlantic right whales until they had almost completely disappeared. By 1935, when they were given international protection as an endangered species, some scientists suspected there were fewer than 100 right whales left in the North Atlantic Ocean. Most thought the right whale was doomed to extinction.

▼ Copepods, collected by dragging a fine-meshed plankton tow net through the ocean.

Our discovery of a group of right whales that included calves was a sign of hope for the species. In the years that followed, research teams from the New England Aquarium returned to the Bay of Fundy each summer to study the whales. They learned that the bay is the summer and fall nursery ground for most right whale mothers and their new calves in the North Atlantic. There, strong tidal currents mix cold water and nutrients into a rich soup that supports large amounts of right whale food, including copepods, which are their favorite food. Copepods are tiny crab-like animals that live their entire lives drifting in the ocean currents. In the Bay of Fundy, swarms of these animals, each about the size of a grain of rice, form dense underwater clouds. The clouds are so thick that the right whales just open their gaping jaws to feast.

Many different species of whale **migrate**, or travel, between winter breeding and calving grounds and summer feeding grounds. Migration is one way in which animals have adapted to changes in the seasons, and it is common in birds, herding mammals, whales, and many fishes. In whales, most summer migrations move into productive northern waters, where the food is abundant. In the winter, pregnant females move southward, so that when they give birth, their calves can spend their first weeks of life in warmer water.

Our discovery of right whales in the Bay of Fundy had shown us the northern, or "summer," end of the right whale's migration, but we still didn't know where the southern end might be. It took a look back over a hundred years to give us a clue.

▼ Right whales in the Bay of Fundy. Head (*left*), flukes (*center*), and *breaching*, or leaping from the water (*right*).

## The Right Feeding Habits

A right whale does not use teeth to chew food but instead has a mouth full of long, finely fringed plates called *baleen*. The baleen plates are made of a substance similar to a person's fingernails. There are approximately 225 of them, each eight to nine feet long. When the whale swims with its mouth open, the baleen works like a strainer, collecting copepods, juvenile krill, and other tiny ocean creatures. To swallow, the whale probably licks the food off the baleen plates and into its throat by using its gigantic tongue. An adult right whale needs approximately 2,200 to 5,500 pounds of food each day. During feeding, it might dive from 8 to 12 minutes at one time.

▲ Baleen inside the mouth of a dead beached whale.

▼ A right whale feeding on surface, with baleen visible inside its open mouth.

▲ This logbook page from the whaling ship *John and Edward* is dated December 25, 1855, and is like the one that helped the team from the New England Aquarium locate right whales off the coast of Georgia. Above the pictures of the whale are the initials of the small boats that left the ship to harpoon whales. The drawing or stamp of the right whale shows that one whale was killed. The numeral 100 refers to the quantity of oil that the whale produced when its blubber was boiled. To the right of the whale is the ship's position (longitude and latitude). Logbooks also recorded the weather conditions, ship sightings, crew changes, and mutinies.

In 1983, researchers Randy Reeves and Edward Mitchell found the missing piece of the puzzle. Searching through the logbooks of nineteenth-century whaling ships, they discovered that in the winter of 1876 a whaling schooner from New Bedford, Massachusetts, named **Golden City** had pulled into Brunswick, Georgia. It went there to remove its cargo, which included whale oil and whalebone (another name for baleen) from humpback whales taken near the Bahamas. But that year, instead of continuing farther north, as it usually did, the **Golden City** remained around Georgia for a couple of months. While it was there, the crew captured a single right whale.

They must have seen more because the following year a second whaling vessel appeared in Brunswick, and by 1880 five whaling vessels had made Brunswick their winter headquarters. Records showed that at least 25 to 30 right whales were killed there between 1876 and 1882.

In modern times, right whales had occasionally washed up dead along the coast of the southeastern United States, but there had been few sightings of live whales in the area. Even so, if right whales appeared off the coast of Georgia during the winters over a hundred years ago, as the whaling logs suggested, there was a chance they might still do so today. Perhaps Stars, Stripe, and the other right whales we had discovered in the Bay of Fundy traveled there during their seasonal migrations. But to prove it, we would need to survey the area—and we would need a way to recognize and follow individual right whales.

▶ This drawing from the inside cover of an old logbook kept during a voyage to the Indian and Pacific oceans between 1837 and 1839 aboard the whaling ship *Alexander Barclay* shows the harpooning of a whale. Whalers were sometimes pulled along at great speeds in their boats by the ropes attached to harpooned whales. Whalers called this a "Nantucket sleigh ride."

▲ Starry Night.

One of the most important tasks of our yearly surveys in the Bay of Fundy was to collect right whale "mug shots." Photographs and drawings showing callosities, scars, and other distinctive markings were combined to produce identification files for hundreds of individual whales. Together with other research teams studying whales, we began assembling a right whale catalog. The catalog would enable us to recognize individual whales and build up a picture of their movements.

Stars and Stripe were two of the earliest entries in the catalog. Snowball was another. A circular scar on the side of Snowball's head made him look as if he had been hit with a snowball. Stumpy, Droopy, Admiral, Smoothie, Starry Night, Kleenex, Necklace, Baldy, and Spitball were just a few of the other names we came up with in the beginning. Most names fit a feature of the whale that bore its name.

Nancy Gunnlaugsson          10/5/82

Scott Kraus          10/1/89

Laurel Code          10/3/85

Kathy Hazard          9/18/82

Number: _____ 1028 _____
Name: _____ STARRY NITE _____
Year of Birth: _____
Sex: _____ Male _____
Comments: _____
_____
_____

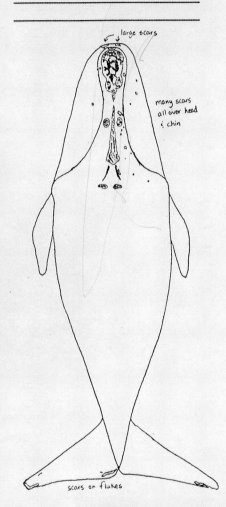

large scars

many scars all over head & chin

scars on flukes

Nancy Gunnlaugsson          10/5/82

# The Right Whale Catalog

Information about North Atlantic right whales has been continually collected over the last few decades by scientists at Woods Hole Oceanographic Institution in Massachusetts, Marineland of Florida, the University of Rhode Island, the Center for Coastal Studies in Provincetown, Massachusetts, and the New England Aquarium. In 1986, these researchers established the North Atlantic Right Whale Consortium. Their goal was to consolidate their research and integrate their photographic collections to create one unified catalog of identified individual right whales. The catalog now contains more than 320 individual whales. The whales, identified by their natural markings, or callosities, and sometimes by their scars, are described in a diagram and by reference photographs taken by researchers. The catalog entry shown here is for Starry Night, the whale pictured on the opposite page. Scientists are not the only contributors to the right whale catalog. Sailors on commercial ships, fishermen, and people in sailboats and other recreational vessels send photographs of right whales to the New England Aquarium. There, three researchers working independently compare the sighting photographs with the catalog entries. If all three match the photograph with the same catalog entry, then the sighting is "officially" recorded in the catalog.

◀ Dave Mattingly (*third from left*) with fellow volunteer pilots.

▶ Whale mother and calf, photographed from the air.

The catalog gave us our breakthrough in solving the puzzle of the right whale migrations. In 1983, at the end of a summer observing right whales in the Bay of Fundy, volunteer Kathy Lindbergh was reviewing a film we had received from the Georgia Department of Natural Resources. The film, taken the previous winter, showed a mother right whale and her calf swimming off the shores of Brunswick, Georgia.

Trying to match whales' faces in photos or film is often tedious and difficult work. But that day we were lucky: in the film, Kathy saw a whale we had seen that summer off the coast of Maine. It was the first time a right whale had been identified in both the northern feeding grounds off the Bay of Fundy **and** in the area off the coast of Georgia.

The findings in the whaling records and Kathy's match between Georgia and Maine were two pieces of evidence that the warm waters along the southeastern United States coast were the right whales' winter calving grounds. We decided to carry out a full-scale survey of the area to see if right whales were calving there.

As luck would have it, in the fall of 1983, Dave Mattingly, a professional airline pilot, called my office to volunteer his services. He was able to organize a group of pilots with private aircraft and flying time to carry out the survey off the coasts of Georgia and Florida. Most people thought we were crazy. No one had searched for right whales in the area since whalers left the region nearly 100 years earlier. When Dave told his friends he was looking for right whales off the coast of Georgia, people looked at him as if he had said he was going to downtown Atlanta to look for dinosaurs.

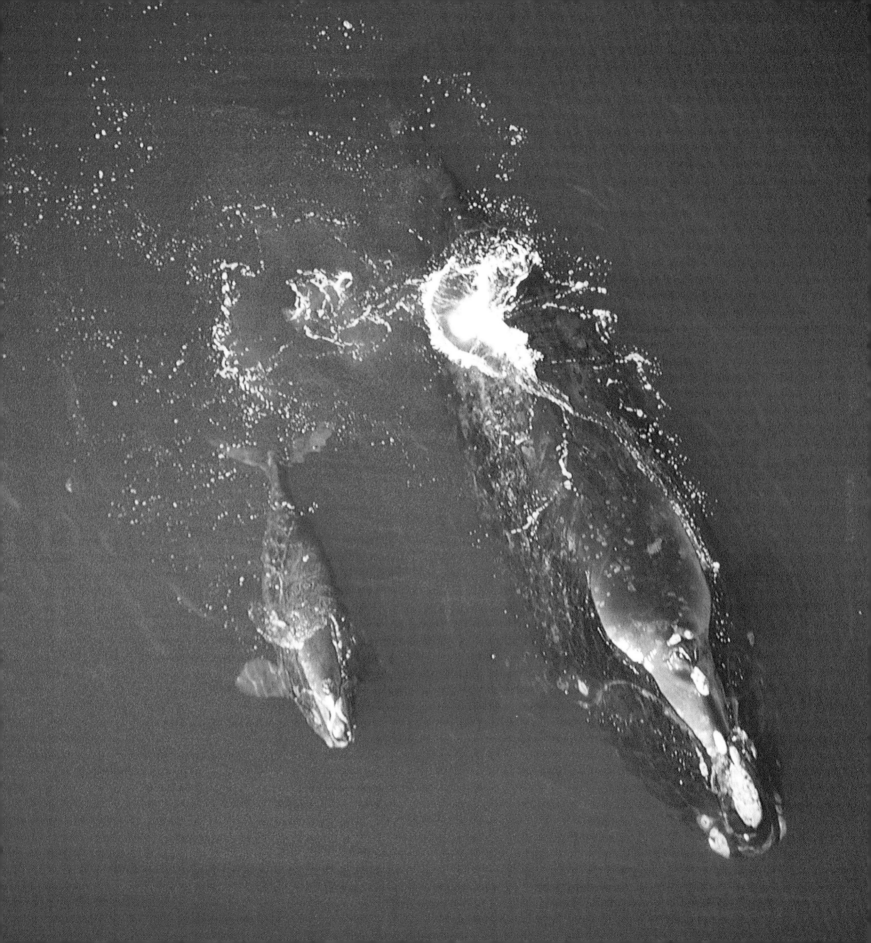

The survey took place in February 1984. Each plane had four people on board. One person flew the plane, one took notes, and the other two acted as observers, whose jobs were to find whales. We flew in a pattern that crossed back and forth in lines, or "tracks," over a section of the ocean, as if we were mowing a lawn. If there were any whales to be seen, this method would increase our chances of finding them.

▼ A pontoon plane lands on the water for a closer look at a whale spotted by a crew member. *Inset:* One of the survey planes above the Florida coast.

It wasn't until the second day that we saw anything except turtles and sharks. Halfway through that day's flights, pilot Jon Hanson tapped me on the shoulder to say he had spotted something in the distance. When we flew in for a closer look, it turned out to be a mother and a baby right whale.

By the end of three days of flying, we had counted 13 right whales, including three mothers with their newborn calves. They were all swimming in coastal waters near the border of Georgia and Florida. One of the mother whales was our old friend Stripe. With her was her fourth calf, Forever. From her size, Forever might have been about two months old.

Since that first survey, our research team and the volunteer pilots have repeated surveys every winter but one. Based on this work and on searches carried out by boat, we know that the coastal waters of Georgia and Florida are the primary calving ground for the entire North Atlantic right whale population.

With the help of the right whale catalog, we have made many photographic matches between whales in the calving grounds and whales seen in the Bay of Fundy and in other places along the North American coast. These matches and surveys, combined with the work of other researchers in Massachusetts and Rhode Island, have begun to provide a picture of the yearly movements of the right whales along the Atlantic coast.

▲ ▶ Two photos showing a southern right whale mother and calf underwater. The calf is between one and three months old.

From December to March of each year, female right whales give birth off the southeastern United States coast. Mothers and calves stay close together, usually apart from other mothers and calves. After its birth—tail first and underwater—the newborn calf does little except eat, play, and rest. It feeds from two nipples hidden in slits along its mother's belly. The milk provides all the nourishment the baby needs. Whale milk is so rich in fat that a newborn right whale may gain a ton—2,000 pounds—in little over a month.

With the arrival of warmer weather and increasing daylight during the spring, mothers and calves begin a 1,400-mile journey north along the Atlantic coast. They stay close to each other because the calf is still very dependent on its mother's milk. But if they do get separated, we think they use underwater moos and squeals to help them keep in touch.

By April and sometimes earlier, the first of the right whale mothers and calves arrive in waters off the Massachusetts coast. Throughout the winter and during their journey north, the female whales have been living off the fat they store in their blubber. But as they reach cooler waters, they begin to feed. Researchers have observed right whales feeding in the Great South Channel–a deep water passage between the tip of Cape Cod and a productive underwater fishing bank 60 miles to the east called Georges Bank–and in Massachusetts Bay. By the end of July they reach the Bay of Fundy and continue their feast. The whales we have observed in the Bay of Fundy remain there for as long as three months.

▼ Spitball, photographed off the coast of the southeastern United States.

# Right Whale Migration

The broad green arrow shows the general pattern of right whale migration: from the coastal waters off Florida and Georgia (the "Georgia Bight") north to feeding grounds in the Great South Channel and Massachusetts Bay, and on to breeding and nursery areas in the Bay of Fundy and Browns Bank (*see pages 30-33*). The red arrow shows sightings of one particular whale, Stars, during 1989.

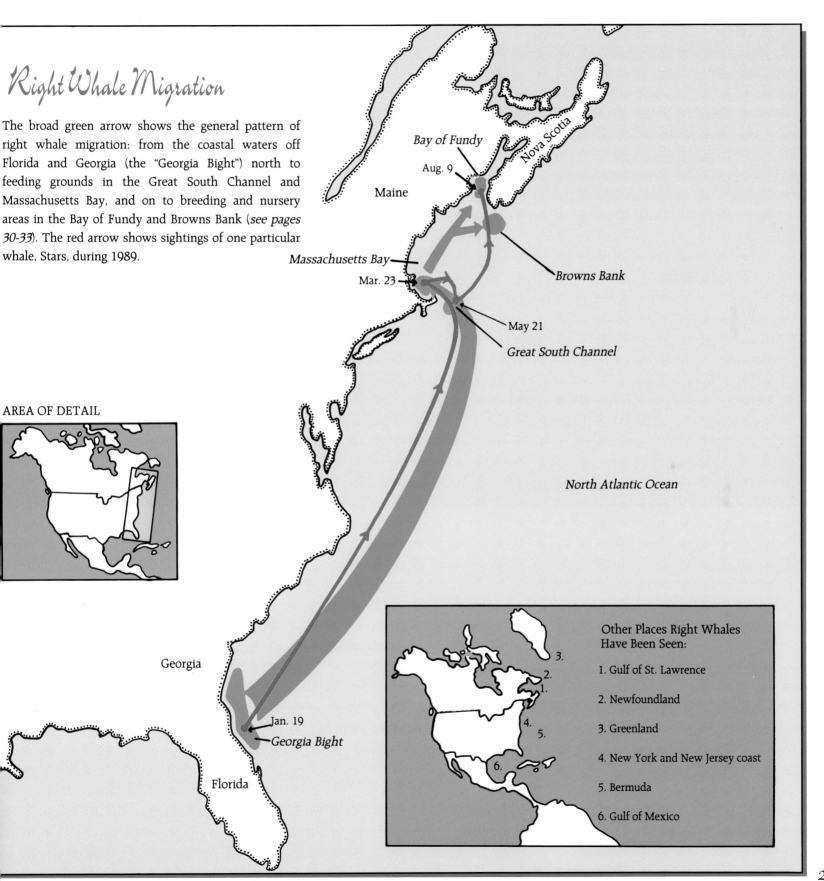

AREA OF DETAIL

Bay of Fundy

Aug. 9

Maine

Nova Scotia

Massachusetts Bay

Mar. 23

Browns Bank

May 21

Great South Channel

North Atlantic Ocean

Georgia

Jan. 19
Georgia Bight

Florida

Other Places Right Whales Have Been Seen:

1. Gulf of St. Lawrence

2. Newfoundland

3. Greenland

4. New York and New Jersey coast

5. Bermuda

6. Gulf of Mexico

The whales need a lot of luck to make the 1,400-mile journey successfully. They travel the same route north as cargo vessels and passenger ships. We know of at least six right whale deaths since 1970 because of collisions with ships. The whales also have to contend with fishing nets. At least three right whales have become entangled in fishing gear and drowned in the last 20 years. Another 11 right whales—including Stars—have been observed swimming with ropes and nets from fishing gear trailing off them. Furthermore, over half the population have scars from entanglements— causing us to wonder if more deaths have occurred than we've heard about.

▲ The scar on this whale was
probably caused by a ship's propeller.

▲ Stars, with fishing gear caught in
her baleen.

By the summer of 1986, six years after our discovery of right whales in the
Bay of Fundy, we had solved part of the puzzle of the right whale's migration.
We knew that most females with calves spent their summers feeding in the
Bay of Fundy and their winters in the calving grounds off the coasts of Georgia
and Florida. But part of the puzzle was still missing: Where did the females
**without** calves and most of the male whales go? That was made a little clearer
by our surveys in another right whale gathering place, this time far off the
coast of Nova Scotia.

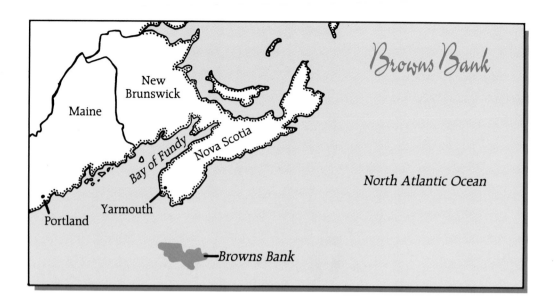

Late in August 1986, I sailed from Yarmouth, Nova Scotia, aboard the fishing boat **Melissa Marie**, under the command of fishing master Delphis Doucette. We had chartered his boat to take us out to an area near Browns Bank, a shallow fishing ground south of the southern tip of Nova Scotia. Howard Winn of the University of Rhode Island had organized airplane surveys of this area in the early 1980s and reported right whale sightings, and we wanted to find out whether it might be a summer feeding ground for adult right whales. Delphis Doucette wasn't convinced. He laughed at first, because he had never seen many whales there. The next two days left him shaking his head in astonishment.

▼ Photographing whales at Browns Bank. The whale in the foreground o the picture on the left has fishing gear caught in its mouth.

By the end of the second day of our survey, when it began to get too dark
to take pictures, we had photographed nearly 70 different whales. We tried
to make an accurate count, but we were overwhelmed. In this relatively
small area, about four miles in diameter, we estimated that there were over
100 right whales.

The whales were diving and feeding on the rich soup of copepods in the cold water. More exciting for us, however, was that they were also involved in courtship and mating. We counted 19 "courtship groups," one with at least 20 whales in it. In these groups, there is usually a single female, surrounded by males. The female appears to call to the males. The males compete for the opportunity to mate with her by pushing one another, by holding on to the female, and by resisting the attempts of other males to displace them. By creating such a competitive situation, the female is making sure that the male that manages to stay with her the longest is probably the "fittest" father for her calves.

Since 1986 we have returned to Browns Bank to conduct yearly surveys. We now believe that Browns Bank is the North Atlantic right whale's primary breeding ground and the place where most adults without calves migrate to during the summer months.

We still don't know where the males and females without calves go year after year during the winter. Most of the North Atlantic is a wilderness of ocean, untraveled except for the fishing and cruising boats that pass from time to time. Imagine a population of right whales numbering only a few hundred scattered over thousands of square miles of ocean and you have an idea of how difficult a task it will be for us to find them. In the meantime, the search for the right whale is a race against time.

Despite protection from whaling for more than 50 years, the population of North Atlantic right whales is growing very slowly, with perhaps no more than 350 alive today. Right whales are threatened by collisions with ships, entanglements in certain types of fishing gear, and pollution. And with such a small population, there is also the possibility that inbreeding will lead to genetic defects and further endanger the species' survival.

▶ A courtship group. The male in the foreground has just rolled over on his back to dive under the female.

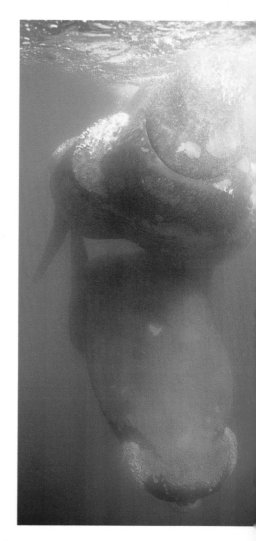

▶ Mating southern right whales, photographed underwater. The female is on top and the male beneath, upside down.

## Research and Conservation

In addition to establishing the right whale's migration patterns, in the past three years we have also come to understand much more about right whale history, biology, and conservation. Researchers Amy Knowlton and Jackie Ciano photographically matched whales seen off Greenland with whales seen off Canada, Georgia, and Florida, increasing the known migration range of some right whales by over 1,000 miles.

By analyzing the whales' genetic makeup, Canadian researchers Cathy Schaeffe and Brad White discovered that although there are presently more than 50 right whale mothers giving birth regularly, there was a period in the last 500 years when only three right whale mothers were reproducing. This means that at one time the North Atlantic right whales were so scarce that today's entire population are descended from just three mothers.

Researchers Bob Kenney, Howard Winn, and Stormy Mayo discovered that right whales can locate very small patches of plankton with better precision than our best oceanographic equipment. And Canadian researcher Moira Brown discovered a way to tell males and females apart by analyzing the DNA from a whale's skin.

Another helpful step for the future of the right whales is the "Recovery Plan for the Right Whale," a document produced for the U.S. National Marine Fisheries Service. The plan uses all available surveys and photographic information to identify where right whales live and what needs to be done to protect them. Still, much conservation work needs to be done, and many questions about right whales remain unanswered.

Continued research into the migration and behavior of the right whales is a crucial part of protecting their future. Without this research, we cannot hope to protect their habitat—and without some help protecting their habitat, there is a danger that the North Atlantic right whales may disappear forever from the oceans. As long as we continue to see Stars, Stripe, and Forever during our surveys, however, we know that there is a chance for the survival of the right whale.

# Afterword

What began as a chance discovery in 1980 is still a detective story today. With each passing year, new clues result in more questions than answers. In 1980, our first estimates of the population suggested no more than 350 right whales existed in the North Atlantic. Although today we know over 300 individual right whales through photo identification, our estimate of the population is still 350.

We see new calves and have identified females over 57 years old, but right whales are still on the wrong track. While it was the **right** whale to hunt for more than 1,000 years, the danger is no longer from hunting. Entanglement in fishing gear, collisions with ships, and problems resulting from a loss of genetic diversity all point to the possible extinction of a great whale—the first potential extinction in our time of one of the migratory giants of the open ocean.

Our care and concern for this magnificent creature should not diminish our care and concern for other open ocean species, including tuna and sharks. We have learned that humans have the capability to over-exploit the sea. We must continue our "search for the right whale," but we must also use the lessons we have learned here to prevent the loss of other precious wildlife in the sea.

John Prescott

Executive Director, New England Aquarium

# Index

# About the Authors

**Scott D. Kraus** is an associate scientist at the Edgerton Research Laboratory at the New England Aquarium, in Boston, Massachusetts. He received his master's degree in biology from the University of Massachusetts, Boston, has been a director of the North Atlantic Marine Mammal Association since 1986 and a director of Seafarers Expeditions, Inc., since 1985. He is a charter member of the Society for Marine Mammalogy. Mr. Kraus has published numerous articles, papers, and technical publications, and has been focusing his attention on the problems of right whales, humpback whales, and harbor porpoises for over 15 years. As a faculty member at the College of the Atlantic in Bar Harbor, Maine, and at the Massachusetts Bay Marine Studies Consortium, he has taught lecture, laboratory, and field courses on marine mammals. He lives in the Boston area.

**Kenneth Mallory** is co-author (with Andrea Conley) of *Rescue of the Stranded Whales*, which was named an Outstanding Nature Book for Children by the John Burroughs Association, an International Reading Association Young Adults' Choice, and an Outstanding Science Trade Book for Children by the joint committee of the Children's Book Council and the National Teachers' Association. Other books by him include *The Red Sea* and the forthcoming *Water Hole: Life in a Rescued Tropical Forest*. He is director of publishing at the New England Aquarium, where he also organizes the Lowell Lecture Series and is a contributing editor to *Aqualog*, the Aquarium's newsletter/magazine. He lives in Newton Highlands, Massachusetts.

## Acknowledgments

The research described in this book is the result of more than a decade of contributions and cooperative efforts by many people and organizations. John Prescott of the New England Aquarium, Dr. Bob Kenney and Dr. Howard Winn of the University of Rhode Island, Dr. Stormy Mayo and Marilyn Marx of the Center for Coastal Studies, and Dr. William Watkins and Karen Moore of Woods Hole Oceanographic Institution are the founders and active participants in the North Atlantic Right Whale Consortium. Support for the Consortium efforts has come from the U.S. National Marine Fisheries Service, the U.S. Minerals Management Service, the Army Corps of Engineers, the U.S. Marine Mammal Commission, the World Wildlife Fund (U.S.), the Island Foundation, and the William Alton Jones Foundation.

At the Aquarium, Amy Knowlton, Moira Brown, Jackie Ciano, Martie Crone, Phil Hamilton, Chris Slay, and Al Barker are the foundation of this program's success. Special credit also goes to Jeanne Rankin, Dave Mattingly, Dr. Brad White, Cathy Schaeffe, Greg Stone, and Randy Reeves. This work could not have been done without the efforts of over 100 volunteers and seasonal staff who have worked with us since 1980.